*How Can I Be over the Hill
When I Haven't Seen the Top Yet?*

How Can I Be Over The Hill When I Haven't Seen The Top Yet?

Faith-full Reflections on the Middle Years of Life

PATRICIA WILSON

UPPER
ROOM BOOKS
NASHVILLE

How Can I Be over the Hill When I Haven't Seen the Top Yet?

Cover and Book Design: Jim Moore
Cover Transparency: Lynn Freeny
First Printing: April 1989 (7)
Second Printing: November 1989 (10)
Third Printing: March 1991 (7)
Library of Congress Catalog Card Number: 88-051470
ISBN: 0-8358-0593-X

Printed in the United States of America

*For Ron and June Armstrong,
who know that every age is
the golden age!*

CONTENTS

PREFACE

When my favorite editor, Charla Honea, suggested that I try writing this book from a "middle-aged" perspective, I had a bad moment or two.

Middle-aged? Me? There must be some mistake.

It was an idea that didn't sit comfortably, until I went for lunch with a high-school friend I hadn't seen in twenty years. I expected her to look like the image in my memory, but much to my shock, she was middle-aged!

Suddenly, I realized that I, too, had made that quantum leap from "young" to an age that someone once defined as "over the hill." Well, I don't know how or when I arrived "over the hill," but I can assure you that the view is just as good. No, it's better!

And I can always console myself with the thought that although my physical body seems to be slowly sliding downhill, my spiritual body is renewed daily. In my Christian life, I remain a "babe of Christ."

As for being middle-aged . . . it doesn't bother me anymore. In fact, some of my best friends are middle-aged!

Living in Prime Time

*So get rid of your old self, which made you
live as you used to—the old self that was
being destroyed by its deceitful desires. Your
hearts and minds must be made completely
new, and you must put on the new self, which
is created in God's likeness and reveals itself
in the true life that is upright and holy.*

—Ephesians 4:22-24

ONE

I've never had a "mid-life crisis." I'm beginning to think that I've missed out on that opportunity to relive my adolescent growing pains. I've come close, once or twice. And like a lot of people I know who are currently going through, or have gone through, their own mid-life crises, I've wondered (in a non-focused kind of way) who I am, what I'm doing, and why! I guess it must be that we mid-lifers suddenly realize that it's half-time and we haven't scored a goal in the game yet. It becomes imperative for us to find out why!

It was with this thought in mind that I impulsively signed up for a "Spring Tonic" program offered through a local outreach group. I've never been particularly fond of "group" kinds of encounters, and I suppose if my thoughts had been less inwardly centered, I would have tried some prayer instead. (My favorite tongue-in-cheek adage: Why pray when you can take pills and worry?) However, as always, Jesus took a situation and used it to teach me a little more about me and a lot more about him. "Spring Tonic" proved to be the cure for any impending mid-life crisis I might have had.

There were eight of us in the group, which met in the basement recreation room of Bill Lamb. He was indeed a gift from the Lord with his gentle, loving leadership. We were invited to explore where we were on our faith journey and where we wanted to be. We were encouraged to express our fears, our worries, and our doubts and to bring them to Jesus for healing. One of the moments that remains very clear in my mind is a simple exercise that gave us new insights into our present state of mind.

"If you were a rose," Bill asked, "what kind of rose would you be?"

A rose! I've never in my wildest imagination thought of myself as a rose. A crysanthemum perhaps, or even a tiger lily, but never a rose.

It took some creative visioning to finally decide I was a yellow rose, old and neglected, growing on a brick wall of some forgotten garden. I immediately saw why I had been feeling in the need of some spring tonic.

The response that most sticks in my mind, however, is that of one of the ladies in the group. She exhibited what I call "squeaky Christianity." She was up-tight, buttoned-down, emotionally repressed, joyless, and sad. *If the spirit ever moved her,* I thought, *she would undoubtedly squeak with disuse.*

Her rose? "I am a wild rose," she said, "growing freely beside the fence on some country roadside." She

14

paused, as the picture formed in her mind. "Yes," she sighed wistfully, "I would be wild and free . . . wild and free!" Such longing was in her voice. We prayed that the Loving Liberator would set her spirit free. And he did.

Most mid-life crisis sufferers don't have the opportunity simply to become a rose in God's garden. Desperately, they seek the causes of their present discontents and failures, looking to their pasts for the answers.

Self-help books for the repair of the psyche abound. There are books to scrutinize dreams; books to get in touch with feelings; books for the past, the present, the future. Each offers a solution to the lack of goals scored in life.

They all have the same starting point: "What I am today is because of what I was yesterday." Whatever my failure, a little judicious poking into my past is bound to turn up something I can use as an excuse.

Of course, the navel gazing doesn't stop at the first step of self-discovery. From there, I can leap into all kinds of interesting therapy techniques to help me out.

I can try some primal screaming.

Or dream analysis.

Or transcendental meditation.

Or life regressions.

Or psychoanalysis.

Or chemical experimentation.

Or psychic healing.

Or tarot cards, palmistry, and horoscopes.

And if none of those techniques work, I can always blame it on my past experiences. "Nothing ever works for me anyway."

The trouble with this kind of excuse is that it is self-defeating. It's as if we prepare ourselves for the race of life by tying lead weights around our ankles.

I used to run my own particular race that way. My father deserted Mother and me when I was nine years old (in an age when such things were not the norm), and for many years, I had a myriad of excuses to use whenever I was faced with a situation that caused me any degree of anxiety, particularly in the area of relationships.

I pretended that I didn't need anyone or anything. I had to be self-sufficient—I was an only child, a precursor of the latchkey kids of today. I couldn't trust another person (except my mother), because I had such a strong feeling of being deserted by my father. I couldn't admit that I wanted to be protected or spoiled or taken care of—that was for the weak.

I was a "liberated" woman long before it was fashionable, but not by choice. I felt that my past circumstances had forced me into a mold that I could never escape.

Until I met Jesus. He freed me from my past, allowed me to become fully human. I could love openly, without fear of hurt or rejection, and be loved in return. Whenever I felt the encroachment of my past experiences, I simply reminded myself that I had been made new. The past of my old self was no longer relevant in my new life as a Christian.

Easy to say, but not easy to put into practice. The only solution is to allow the Lord to wipe the slate clean for me. When I find myself blaming some past experience for my present failure, I need to ask the Lord to erase that experience from my memory banks. Then that particular tape can no longer be replayed, and it is up to me, with the Lord's help, to create new, positive tapes for my life.

I can never go back. The road ahead of me leads in one direction only—onward. Whether I choose to detour onto past excuses or press ahead depends on my determination to reach the goal. The Christian life is a one-way street.

TWO

Is the View Just as Good from over the Hill?

For this reason we never become discouraged. Even though our physical being is gradually decaying, yet our spiritual being is renewed day after day.

—2 Corinthians 4:16

TWO

Most of the time, I don't notice that I'm growing older. In some far recess of my mind, my biological clock seems to have stopped at thirty-three years. My mental self-image has no gray in her hair, the wrinkles haven't taken hold, and her chin is still singular.

Occasionally, I catch a glimpse of a much older woman in the bathroom mirror, but I just put that down to bad lighting. When I meet the parents of my children's friends, I am always surprised at how old they look. ''Must have started late,'' I tell myself, ignoring the fact that I was a late-blooming parent myself. And if the policeman who stops my car at the roadcheck seems young enough to be my son, I just assume that he's a new recruit.

All in all, I feel that I have my aging process pretty well under control.

Until, that is, I met Betty again. Betty and I had attended elementary school together and high school after that. Even when we parted to go our separate ways—she to teachers' college and I to a technical school—we still kept in touch. Then we moved on to our own lives and careers. Briefly, we met again when I was a bridesmaid at her wedding, and several months later she came to mine. We didn't meet again for over twenty years, although we did occasionally exchange notes and change-of-address cards.

Through the usual kind of corporate moves, she and her family ended up in Ottawa. To our mutual delight, I was now living a scant hour's drive away. We had never been physically closer. A reunion was in order.

We agreed to meet on our own first, before we brought our families together. It seemed fairer to get all of our "Do you remembers . . ." out of the way. Neither of us felt we had to wear a rose in our lapel to distinguish us from the crowd. We'd know each other anywhere!

When I arrived, I asked the maitre d' whether Mrs. St. Onge was there yet. She wasn't. I settled back to wait.

Then, Betty's mother came through the door! Well, it wasn't Betty's mother . . . it was Betty. Somehow, I hadn't expected her to look a bit different from my old school friend. I certainly hadn't expected her to look—how can I put it delicately?—middle-aged!

After all, I hadn't changed. Why should she? Then I saw Betty staring at me in the same open-mouthed surprise. Could it be that I now looked like *my* mother?

Impossible! Could it be that I was also middle-aged? Unthinkable!

Betty and I easily picked up where we had left off twenty years earlier. Only now, we were both aware of the richness and fullness of our lives . . . lives that had been through joys and sorrows; lives that had experienced grief and pain, happiness and contentment, peace and hope and faith. We were so much *more* of what we had been in our youth. Looking back, those young girls were mere shadows of the women we had become.

And when we joked about being middle-aged, it was with a sense of anticipation: only halfway through and so much more living to be done. Suddenly, I didn't mind those few gray hairs, the extra inches on my middle, the soft chinline, the laughter lines around my eyes. They were my badges of honor, the proof that I had *lived* my life fully.

The world doesn't see it that way. We've been told that we must hide our aging process at any cost. I simply have to open a magazine, flip through the catalogue, or turn on the television. There "they" are, waiting for me, those goddesses of youth disguised as young, eternally perfect women. They parade in never-ending diversity before me, exquisitely groomed, perfectly dressed, and look like a stop-frame picture of the me I used to dream of being.

Not only do they look wonderful, they brag about it. Without a flicker of embarrassment, they tell me that only their hairdresser knows for sure, that their age is a secret that keeps others guessing, that they can't pinch an inch on any part of their torso, and that it's expensive, but they're worth it.

They charge through their high-powered business meetings sustained only by their high-powered pantyhose. They greet their families at breakfast wearing cashmere sweaters and pearls. They emerge from a two-hour workout with just the teensiest glow of perspiration on their upper lip. They don't seem to worry about sagging chinlines, disappearing waistlines, or thinning hair. Varicose veins, orthopedic shoes, and Ben-Gay have no part in their world. And I'll bet my last corn-plaster that they don't share a bathroom with a husband, two teenagers, and various cats and dogs who wander through just to see what they're up to.

They are blatantly self-centered, these beautiful doyennes of youth, and they don't care who knows it. In their lives, aging is a battle to be won or lost.

There is a glimmer of self-pity in their perfectly mascaraed eyes as they tell me that they're not growing old gracefully; they're fighting it every inch of the way! No doubt they know who is in their admiring audience— women like me who think that having time to trim their toenails once every two weeks is the height of self-indulgence; women like me who still cut their hair with the kitchen scissors; women like me who can pinch inches on their double chins alone.

Where is it written that aging is a battle? Where did we get the idea that growing older was something to be avoided at all costs? Who decided that young was beautiful and anything older than young was unacceptable? When did age become a liability?

Is it some kind of superplot hatched up by cosmetic company owners and model agencies? In a society whose fastest growing population segment is over forty, we seem to have put the cart before the horse, so to speak. Instead of emphasizing the mature look, the beauty of an older face, the comforting curves of a less-than-lean body, we insist that we all become Peter Pans and refuse to grow up or grow older. Age is no longer a factor of value, but a secret that must be hidden at all costs. We are a society which believes that, unlike fine wine or precious antiques, our value decreases with age.

I don't really like growing older, mind you. I resent the inability of my body to bounce back from a late night, and I find it difficult to accept my increasing aches and pains. Where I used to work cheerfully in the garden all day, I now have to pace myself or suffer backache as a consequence. I don't like being told by a doctor who is still wearing braces on his teeth, ''You're not getting any younger, you know,'' and I don't like having to remember to take my vitamins in the winter and put on my sunscreen in the summer. Getting older seems to mean more and more maintenance of the general body plant.

———————

I'm glad that my spiritual body is a lot easier to maintain. In fact, it becomes stronger each day that I walk with the Lord. Unlike my earthly shell that reaches a peak and then slides inexorably downhill, my spiritual body continues ever onward and upward.

As I use my spiritual gifts, I can feel them strengthen and sustain me. My faith deepens; my hope grows; my peace abides. The spiritual body thrives on daily use.

And the view just gets better and better on the upward journey!

THREE

Do You Smell Smoke?

You must remove the old yeast of sin so that you will be entirely pure. Then you will be like a new batch of dough without any yeast, as indeed I know you actually are.

—*1 Corinthians 5:7*

THREE

One of the advantages of being around for a while is that I have finally become quite proficient in the kitchen. In fact, when I think back to the first meal I prepared as a young bride—wieners and cabbage (obviously in a presensitive-stomach age)—I can truly say that I have come a long way. Years of practice have given me a reputation as a good cook.

On the other hand, my housekeeping skills have not improved over the years. No one has ever been able to eat off my kitchen floor, although I've always wondered who would want to do that in the first place. My cupboards are in an organized state of chaos: organized because I can always find what I want, and chaos because nobody else can. My refrigerator has a number of life-forms of its own, the most notable of which can usually be found in either the cheese container or the vegetable bins. At any given time, I can pretty well guarantee that the garbage needs taking out, the dishwasher needs emptying, or the sink needs scrubbing.

Few complain, however, because good things come out
of my kitchen. I may be messy, but not dirty; untidy, but
not disgusting. My family knows that the disorder is only
skin deep, and eventually, in a fit of Ms. Clean, I'll get
the whole works back to rights.

Except, of course, for my stove. I hate stoves. They
are dirty, messy, smelly things, invented by some sadistic
fellow who had it in for cooks. The burners have been
cunningly designed so that every drip runs into little
crannies and bakes hard as a rock in tiny, inaccessible
places. And ovens! Horrid great caverns that encourage
pans of anything to run over onto the heating element, or
force anything with fat in it to spatter all over the sides
and end up as a smoking puddle in the bottom.

I'm supposed to believe it is all easily curable as I
watch some lady on television trot out in a silk blouse
and pearls, wipe on some miracle goo, and just as easily
wipe it off with her lace handkerchief. Presto—a shining
clean stove with nary a spot to show for its previous
state. Hah!

Six hours, four rolls of paper towels, two buckets of
soapy water, and a gallon of miracle goo later, my stove
has lost its first layer of black glop. I have lost the first
layer of skin on my hands.

Frankly, it's just not worth it. Forget the miracle goo. I
have found a solution that's a lot easier on the hands and
on the pocketbook (have you seen how much that miracle
goo costs?). Leave the whole mess. Nature eventually

takes care of the problem for you. In six months or so, the whole business in the bottom of the oven bakes into little charcoal flakes that you can brush out with a handbroom. Of course, it doesn't look all shiny and clean, but it doesn't look that way after my assault with the oven cleaner, either.

There is one small flaw in my oven-cleaning scheme. During the carbonization process (fancy words for slow burn), some residual smoke and smell emanates from the oven every time you turn it on. This is no problem if you have a properly trained family used to this kind of thing. In our house, a little smoke merely indicates that the cook is hard at work in the kitchen.

However, you do run into problems shortly after a major meltdown, say the residual effects of a pork roast, scalloped potatoes, and pudding in the oven, and brown sugar sauce and pan gravy on the burners.

The next meal, although appetizing once it has reached the plates, is definitely not so while the cooking process is going on. Regardless of whether it's sirloin steak or hamburgers, its tantalizing aroma is masked by the heavy smell of carbonizing culinary masterpieces.

Worse, the smoke usually billows up in a black, thick cloud that quickly spreads throughout the house.

"What's that awful smell?" someone hollers down.

"Just Mom cooking" comes the complacent reply.

No problem if it's only family around, but I have found that my guests tend to get a little twitchy after being served a meal that began with black smoke and disgusting smells. Sometimes, if the smell is particularly pungent, even the cook loses her appetite.

Funny how last week's pork roast can spoil this week's turkey.

———————

I wish life could be like my oven. It would be a lot easier if I could leave the whole mess to eventually burn off. I'd even be willing to live with a few nasty smells in the meantime.

Unfortunately, all those little things I've never forgotten (or forgiven)—the petty arguments, the spiteful gossip, the hurtful remarks—remain like crusted ashes on the surface of my heart. Years later, their dank smoke and odor can still spoil the flavor of my daily spiritual life.

Unlike the massive undertaking my oven requires, the spiritual ashes of my past angers are more easily removed: a moment to identify the smell; a moment to ask the Lord to ''soften'' up the crust with divine love; and a moment to let the ashes blow away.

I don't even have to get my hands dirty!

Always Check the Label First

But you are the chosen race, the King's priests, the holy nation, God's own people, chosen to proclaim the wonderful acts of God, who called you out of darkness into his own marvelous light.

—1 Peter 2:9

FOUR

I have always presumed that child-raising would be-come easier as both the child and I matured. Although my mother used to threaten me with, "I hope you have a a teenager just like yourself," I never really believed that teenagers would be a real problem. After all, my memo-ries of my own teen years were rosy ones.

Now, with two of the species living in the same house with me, I often wish that even one of them was the least bit like the teenager I remember being: helpful, cheerful and, most of all, undemanding.

I don't remember insisting on a particular kind of garment and refusing to wear anything else. Oh yes, I do have vague memories of expressing a mild desire for white bucks (shoes) rather than the oxfords my mother offered, and perhaps I did show some interest in bunny bows (fluffy pompoms on the end of a velvet string), but I'm sure I never made an issue of these passing whims.

Not so with my daughter. Cherith has become a veritable tyrant. Not to mention the expert on what's "in" as opposed to what's "out." "In" is always identified by the label. No substitutes will suffice. For Cherith, The Label is the only criteria for acceptance.

In all the manuals on child-raising that I have ever read, I have never found a chapter on anything that even vaguely resembles what I call "Label Worship." Yet, my conversations with other parents have confirmed my suspicion that this cult is running rampant among our young people. It seems to start shortly after they are able to repeat brand names from television commercials and reaches its critical stage when they enter their teen years.

Its gods, with names like Reebok, Cardin, Levi, and Esprit, demand sacrifices of hard-earned dollars, lots of them and often. They are gods with whims that shift with every passing fashion breeze. Last year's sacrifice for the red-banded, extra-heavy, superinsulated, custom model is not acceptable for this year. This year, a sacrifice must be made for the green-spotted, lightweight, double-lined, high-style model. Nothing less will suffice.

These gods have Madison Avenue executives as their high priests. Slick advertising campaigns, catchy slogans, bouncy jingles, great gimmicks form the liturgy.

Label worship in our house reached a peak after Cherith enrolled in modeling school. Now she had a roomful of peers, equally committed to the cult, who passed on the names of their own particular gods. If I had thought that clothes were the epitome of Labeling, I was in for a rude awakening.

Labeled make-up took the worship to new heights of devotion. Only hyperallergenic imported makeup, composed of rare ingredients, found only in exclusive (read expensive) salons, would do. Hairspray had to be French, body lotion Italian, and nothing could come from Woolworth's.

I decided it was time to do some de-programming.

I started by dragging my protesting daughter to places with names like Bargain Bob's Bonanza Barn and Wild Willy's Super Sales Emporium. I insisted that she try on some of the clothes. Usually, we found an item or two that fit. I ignored the look of disdain on her face as she checked the label on the goods. I let her know that I would be doing spot checks to ensure that these items were worn. I threatened to throw out everything else in her closet. It worked, but believe me, I'll never win the Mom of the Year Award with these tactics.

When I see Cherith in the local shopping mall (the chief place of worship) on Saturday (the high holy day), shuffling from store to store, ritually checking labels, comparing labels, coveting labels, I realize that my feeble efforts are futile. How can Bargain Bob and I compete with the tempting displays of neon, chrome, and light?

Where in her upbringing did I go so terribly wrong that Cherith is susceptible to the charms of the label cult? I can't imagine where she got the idea that you should always check the label first!

Or can I?

I'm uncomfortable when I remember the times that I haven't approved of a playmate because he or she doesn't come from the same kind of background that we do.

I'm uncomfortable when I realize that I have judged more than one person by outward appearance. I may not have said anything, but did my attitude show my feelings toward someone who was inappropriately dressed—perhaps wearing jeans to church?

I'm uncomfortable when I think of the times I have made a decision about people based on the way they talk. Have I tended to talk differently to those I think are uneducated?

I'm uncomfortable when I recognize that I have reacted to people whose ways of expressing their love for Jesus have been different from mine. Have I subconsciously dismissed them as fanatics?

Frightening, isn't it? When you begin to look at the ramifications of the label cult, you realize that its effect is more significant than simply the names on goods we choose to buy.

We label our churches, our neighborhoods, and our lifestyles. We even label people.

Then, before we make any kind of commitment, we always check the label first.

If we live in a world that always checks the label first, I should wear my Christian label as proudly as any designer brand. It marks me as a product of grace, and simply says, "His."

However, I tend to tuck my label away somewhere deep inside, where it is visible only to the select few. This protects me from having to live up to the promises of the "His" label. I can forget to love, to forgive, or to hope.

How different my Christian witness would be if I wore that label prominently displayed for all the world to check! In much the same way that the sight of a coveted designer label arouses desire for ownership in the hearts of label cult members, think of the longings I would arouse in others who would see in me the love of Jesus they so desperately need. The "His" label displayed in my life could be a beacon to the empty lives I meet each day.

Time for a Refill

Give to others, and God will give to you. Indeed, you will receive a full measure, a generous helping, poured into your hands—all that you can hold.

—*Luke 6:38*

FIVE

I can remember the horrible sinking feeling in the pit of my stomach as I drove down the highway one Sunday morning and a red light on the dashboard came on.

I don't know much about cars, but I do know that any unexpected light flashing on the dashboard means trouble, usually of a terminal kind. Gauges begin to register danger zones, and funny smells seep in from the engine. I tend to ignore a lot of warning signals in my life, but not red lights on my dashboard.

I stopped at the next gas station, convinced that my car was about to either burst into flames or expire with one final groaning cough.

The young lad at the gas pumps was singularly unimpressed. A quick examination under the hood pinpointed the trouble.

"Radiator's leaking," he told me.

"Can you fix it?"

"Nope. No mechanics on duty on Sunday."

"Can I drive it like this?"

"Well, I wouldn't. Probably burn out the engine. Cost you a bundle to repair. Better leave it here." He turned to the next car in line and began to pump gas.

I said a small, desperate prayer.

The owner of the car behind me got out and walked over. I explained my dilemma to him, wondering what I was going to say if this perfect stranger were to offer me a ride somewhere. How far is this faith stuff supposed to go?

He didn't offer me a lift; he offered me a small yellow plastic bottle from his glove compartment. It had "Stop-Leak" emblazoned on the side.

"Pour it in the radiator," he said. "If the hole's not too big, this will plug it until you can get to a radiator shop." Sometimes, prayers are answered in small yellow plastic bottles.

I had never really thought that my spiritual life was anything like my car radiator until one winter night years later.

Despite the frigid temperatures, nearly five hundred people had gathered to hear the beautiful voice of a well-known gospel singer. Most were people like us who had come from suburban churches around the city; some had come by bus; others had walked in from the nearby men's mission. Although the old church belonged to one of the mainline denominations, the sprinkling of "amens" and "hallelujahs" that followed the opening prayer indicated that a good number of the visitors were from the more vocally outspoken denominations.

As the service proceeded, the enthusiasm of the congregation grew. Feet tapped, hands clapped, and arms were upraised. We were treated to a feast of rousing choruses, stirring testimony, and inspired preaching. It seemed as if our souls could not hold another morsel, and the main course was yet to come.

The guest soloist stepped forward and seated herself at the grand piano placed in the middle of the sanctuary. The lights in the church dimmed. A single spotlight shimmered on her white gown and gleamed on her dark skin. The congregation grew still as the first chord echoed around the vaulted ceiling.

She sang, in liquid notes of golden purity, the old, well-loved words, the familiar melodies that brought a tear of remembrance to most eyes. She sang for nearly an hour, one song following another, with no break in the flow of music.

Finally, there was a pause. Before anyone could move, the woman spoke, "The Holy Spirit certainly has been with us tonight." Several soft "amens" agreed with her. "I like to think that I am filled with that Holy Spirit." She smiled at us, and her dark eyes sparkled. "But sometimes I leak."

Before anyone could catch the meaning of her words, she started to sing her closing song:

Fill my cup, Lord,
I lift it up, Lord!
Come and quench this thirsting of my soul;
Bread of heaven, feed me 'til I want no more—
Fill my cup, fill it up and make me whole!

As the last note died into silence, she softly whispered, "If you're empty tonight, come and lift your cup for his filling."

Many went forward for the first time, and many, like me, went up for a refill. Because sometimes I leak, too.

———————

The trouble with this leaking business is that it is so sneaky. I don't even know that it's happening. I just wake up one morning asking myself why I'm so unhappy, or discontented, or depressed, or miserable, or angry, or frustrated, or frightened, or worried, or hurt. Those feelings are like the red light on my dashboard. They warn me that I've leaked.

Then I know that it's time to ask for a refill, to lift my cup and receive what I've been promised: "pressed down, shaken together, running over" blessings (Luke 6:38, RSV).

In the Christian life, the second cup (and the third, and the fourth . . .) is always free!

What Do You Want to Be When You Grow Up?

Now listen to me, you that say, "Today or tomorrow we will travel to a certain city, where we will stay a year and go into business and make a lot of money." You don't even know what your life tomorrow will be! You are like a puff of smoke, which appears for a moment and then disappears. What you should say is this: "If the Lord is willing, we will live and do this or that."

—James 4:13-15

SIX

I've always claimed that I haven't decided what I want to be when I grow up. That's not entirely true. I may not have decided on a career goal, but I certainly had some pretty definite ideas of the direction I expected my life to take.

Years ago, I clipped a poem from a magazine because I thought it was funny. Now, over twenty years later, it is still funny, but in a bittersweet way. The poem tells of fifteen-year-old author Marybeth Kennedy's expectations for the future—"When I am older, I will live a mad, bohemian life on the Continent—" and of the kind of lifestyle she expects to have—"I will be perpetually tanned and ravishing, keeping company with a small, exclusive, talented circle of friends." She knows what her future will be like: "My husband will murmur to me in French as we glide along in our Rolls-Royce," and she knows how she will bring up her children: "And my children will be named Sarah and Jonothan the Vth and will be taken care of by a Miss Billingston, not me."

But her final lines hold the bittersweet flavor:

> Yes, when I'm older I will,
>   I'm sure.
> Yet every so often
> I get this nagging feeling
> That I'm not headed
> in the
> Right Direction.

I know how she feels. Every so often I get this nagging feeling that I'm not headed in the right direction either.

I had planned to be rich or at least comfortably well off. Yet, when I'm sitting at my desk, wondering how I'm going to pay both the taxes and the phone bill, I get this nagging feeling that I'm not headed in the right direction.

I had planned to be thin. Yet, when I'm trying on a size larger than I tried on last month, or struggling to eat nothing but grapefruit and rice for a week, or letting out the seams on my favorite skirt, I get this nagging feeling that I'm not headed in the right direction.

I had planned to be beautiful. Yet, when I'm picking up yet another lotion to erase those brown spots on my hands or trying another facial mask guaranteed to smooth away the wrinkles, I get this nagging feeling that I'm not headed in the right direction.

I had planned to be Mother of the Year. Yet, when my teenagers threaten to either run away from home or call the children's aid society, when their teachers suggest we should have a little chat and when my mother suggests we should have a little chat about them, I get this nagging feeling that I'm not headed in the right direction.

I had planned to be a perfect wife. Yet, when my husband falls asleep while I'm telling him about my plans for redecorating the family room, or fails to mention my new hairstyle, or eats an entire gourmet meal without comment, I get this nagging feeling that I'm not headed in the right direction.

You see what I mean.

I had also planned to live in a spotless house, faultlessly decorated, situated on several acres overlooking a beautiful lake (or alternatively, an ocean shore), set in a veritable Garden of Eden of flowers, manicured lawns, and fruit trees.

I had also planned to have the kind of job that called for boardroom meetings, designer briefcases, and an up-to-date passport.

It all seemed so possible twenty years ago.

The other night I watched Peter, Paul and Mary's twenty-fifth anniversary concert on television. I sang ''Puff, the Magic Dragon'' and ''If I Had a Hammer,'' and I remembered the girl who had first listened to their records and dreamed of the life that was to be. All these years later, she was sitting in the somewhat untidy family room of a half-finished house, surrounded by snoozing cats, holding the hand of her husband (who did not once murmur to her in French). Outside, she could hear her neighbor's dog barking and, from the paddock, the answering bray of one of her donkeys.

Life never seemed better.

The wrong direction turned out to be the right one after all. But it wasn't the direction that I would have chosen.

I have my expectations laid out similarly for my Christian journey. I want it to be smooth and easy; exciting, but not disturbing; predictable yet interesting; and definitely not too challenging. Yet, every so often I get this nagging feeling that I'm not headed in the Right Direction.

Perhaps it is my stubborn insistence on traveling the path that I have chosen, rather than the path chosen for me, that gives rise to these doubts about the direction I'm taking.

When I see what Jesus has been able to do with my life, despite my efforts to shape it to my own expectations, how much more could he do with my Christian walk if I would let him?

Finally, I might be headed in the Right Direction!

It's Not My Fault!

Get rid of all bitterness, passion, and anger. No more shouting or insults, no more hateful feelings of any sort. Instead, be kind and tender-hearted to one another, and forgive one another, as God has forgiven you through Christ.

—Ephesians 4:31-32

SEVEN

I always dread the first ten seconds after my entrance into any gathering. That's how long it takes me to determine whether or not I know anyone in the room and whether or not we'll have anything to say to each other. At one end of the anxiety scale is not knowing a single soul in the room. At the other end is knowing only a single soul, and that soul not very well. Each situation calls for small talk. Long, in-depth discussions I can handle with aplomb, but I'd sooner hide in a corner all night than make small talk.

When I saw Phil waving at me from across the room, I heaved an inward sigh of relief. Although I didn't know Phil very well, I knew that he liked cats. His office was full of them, figuratively speaking. Posters of cats adorned the walls, stuffed cats sat on his chairs, and "catty" paraphernalia littered every available surface. Even his coffee mug was shaped like a cat! Being a cat lover of the first order myself, I knew that we would have at least one subject in common.

No sooner had I joined him than Phil headed for the buffet and left me to chat with his wife, Tina. We talked generally about things like home renovating, living in the country, and raising kids and cats in the city.

"How many do you have?" Tina asked me.

"Well, I had three when Gerald and I were married, and he had five, so we ended up with eight between us."

"Eight! How old were they?"

"My oldest fellow was ten, and Gerald's youngest was just two years old, and the rest fell in between."

She looked suitably impressed. "That must have been quite an adjustment."

"It was. At first, we had a lot of trouble with squabbling and spats, but eventually, they got the pecking order sorted out, and they live together quite amiably now. Of course, there's still a flare-up now and then, but that's to be expected."

She smiled at me warmly. Encouraged, I continued on my discourse. "It's not so bad now that we're down to four of them."

"Down to four!" She looked horrified. "What happened?"

"One of Gerald's boys was really homesick for his family in Montreal, so we agreed he could live with them. That left us seven at home."

She looked sympathetically at me. "You must have really missed him."

"Not really. I was just as glad to get the numbers

56

down." A look of shock flashed across Tina's face. I ignored it and continued. "Anyway, within a short time, nature and attrition took care of the rest."

Tina's voice was warm with sympathy. She shook her head. "You're so brave about it. What happened to the others?"

I realized that she was a cat lover of the highest order. "Then we lost Vinnie—he was one of mine. Gerald found him in the barn, dead as a doorpost. It looked as if he had fallen from one of the rafters. We were kind of surprised because they usually survive that kind of fall, but not poor Vinnie."

Her hand reached over and patted mine. Her brown eyes filled with tears. "It must have been a dreadful experience."

"Actually, I hadn't had Vinnie all that long, so it wasn't too bad. And we still had six left to keep us busy."

Tina's eyes narrowed, and she looked at me in puzzlement. I realized that I should be less flippant in my discussion on the demise of the cats. Trying to settle my face into a suitably somber expression, I continued, "Then one of Gerald's older boys developed a terrible skin disease. We tried everything to cure it—cost us a fortune in medical bills—but in the end, nothing could be done. We finally had to have put him put down."

"Put down!" Her voice mirrored the look of horror on her face.

I began to suspect that Phil's lady was rowing with one oar in the cat-lover's department. I answered her a little sharply. "Well, we didn't have much choice. There's only so much you can do, and then you have to be sensible about these things."

"Sensible!" She started to get up. "I think what you did was awful!"

"Well, so do I, but there comes a time when everyone has to make a decision like this. I had to do the same thing with an old dog of mine, and I cried for days afterward."

At this point, Phil returned from the buffet. "So, are you cat lovers comparing notes?" he asked cheerfully, obviously missing the look on Tina's face.

"We haven't gotten around to cats," Tina said tensely. "And I don't think I want to." She glared at me. "If this is how you treat your children, I'd hate to think of what you would do with your cats!"

―――――――――

It didn't take long for Tina and me to clear up our misunderstanding, perhaps because neither of us minded admitting that we had misunderstood each other.

I wish it were that simple in matters of more serious import. Unfortunately, I don't like to admit that I might have been wrong—that the misunderstanding might actually have been on my part. I'd rather think that the other person made the mistake and should be big enough to admit it.

Some misunderstandings remain "on the books" for years. Always, there is the nagging feeling that I've been foolish and that if I buried my pride long enough to make the first move, the relationship would quickly be restored.

As I grow older, I realize that every relationship is a gift from the Lord, too precious to jeopardize with foolish pride. I make the first move toward reconciliation more readily now.

Those who know me think that I'm getting soft, but I like to think that I've finally become strong enough to admit that a misunderstanding could just possibly have been my fault.

EIGHT

Will the Real "Me" Please Stand Up?

Do not conform yourselves to the standards of this world, but let God transform you inwardly by a complete change of your mind. Then you will be able to know the will of God—what is good and is pleasing to him and is perfect.

—*Romans 12:2*

EIGHT

A year after we bought our initial six chickens and one rooster, we decided it was time to augment our flock. The first birds had come from a bona fide chicken breeder some miles away, but his price and the distance deterred us from making a repeat purchase. I did not relish the thought of another sixty-mile trip with a backseat full of panicky feathered baggage.

We decided that we would look locally for some more birds, and so we were delighted when we saw an ad on the feed-store notice board for "year-old layers" at a bargain price. The voice at the other end of the advertised telephone number assured us that his birds were, like ours, Rhode Island Reds and would lay the same lovely brown eggs. Best of all, his chickens were less than a mile away.

I headed out immediately, determined to bring back a dozen of his finest. I had expected that his chickens also lived in a large airy chicken house and were free to roam the barnyard and fields as they pleased. What I found was a business. The chickens were confined to a small fenced yard, far too small for the hundred or so birds he had.

They had all been debeaked (that is, had the sharp tips of their beaks nipped off shortly after birth) to prevent them from pecking each other to death. The laying boxes were in a dark, smelly shed and were built so that the eggs fell through a slatted bottom into a trough that was opened from the back. The farmer never actually saw his hens laying; he only gathered the product of their labors.

The hens certainly didn't have pet names, distinct personalities, or personal preferences in food. They were simply regarded as laying machines, disposable after their first high-volume year.

"How many do you want?" he asked me.

"A dozen," I said, longing to rescue the whole flock. I started to pick out my dozen lucky ladies, pointing them out behind the wire fence.

"Can't open the yard door," he said. "They'll panic. Pile up in a corner and suffocate each other. We'll get 'em in here."

He led me into the laying shed. Opening the flap doors behind the laying boxes, he unceremoniously grabbed the first unsuspecting hen sitting on the nest. I had no time to inspect my purchase as he stuffed her into a feed bag and reached for the next. Twelve feed bags and twelve dollars later, I was on my way home.

It took several traumatic weeks before our old and new

flocks finally integrated. Soon, except for the clipped beaks, it was difficult to tell one group of hens from the other. Except, that is, for one of the new hens who seemed somehow different from the rest. It wasn't a difference you could actually put your finger on—perhaps she had a little longer chin wattles, and her tail feathers seemed a tad fuller, and her drumsticks a little meatier—but the difference was barely discernible. In all ways she was like the rest; she scratched for worms in the yard, perched next to the rooster at night, and sat on a nest every afternoon.

After some diligent detective work, we discovered that nothing was ever produced as a result of her laying efforts. Now most hens will sit on the nest only when the "urge" to lay strikes them, and many miss a day or two between eggs. But this hen never missed a day. Each afternoon around two, she would climb into a nesting box, doze quietly for an hour, and then rejoin the rest in the yard. She never laid an egg.

I got out my Chicken Manual, and an awful suspicion began to dawn on me. A quick up-turned inspection confirmed our diagnosis. We didn't have a hen. We had a capon—a rooster whose sole purpose is to be fattened for market, a purpose made possible by a "minor" operation. She wasn't a she, and she wasn't a he . . . she was an "it." Somehow, he had been put in with the chicks destined to be laying hens.

We called him "Doubtful," and until the end of his days with us, he continued to be "one of the girls."

―――――――――

Sometimes, I feel like Doubtful. I feel as if I have to take on the protective coloration of the world around me in order to live in it. I become just another one of the rats in the rat race, and I hope that no one notices I am different. I think that I can avoid the stew pot that way.

But my spirit rebells against the worldly mold I try to fit into. Deep inside, it tells me that I am different; that I am called to be separate; that the way I live my life should be a witness to those around me. More important, it tells me that the stew pot of public opinion has no power over me.

The only way I can find my inner peace is to be what I was created to be—a child of God, a follower of Jesus.

I cannot be a Doubtful.

This Must Be the Wrong Garden

But who are you, my friend, to talk back to God? A clay pot does not ask the man who made it, "Why did you make me like this?"

—Romans 9:20

NINE

I always thought that jobs were easy to find. I should
know, since I've had more than just one or two in my
lifetime, and in each case, I've just moved on to the next
one when I've wanted a change.

Until, however, I found myself at a large computer
company in Toronto. The job itself hadn't been too hard
to land, even though it was in a field in which I hadn't
much real experience. I was hired to write the training
manuals for computer software programs. I knew I could
write, and I convinced my new bosses that one kind of
writing was just like another.

Within three days, I knew that I had made a terrible
mistake. I hated the job. I hated the silly computers that
kept telling me, "Invalid entry" and "Input error" and
"Program not found." I hated the reams of computer
printouts that had to be read and interpreted and rewrit-
ten. Most of all, I hated the tedium of a herculean
task—writing pages and pages of instructions that gener-

ally said, "Press space bar" and "Insert any three-digit figure."

Mentally, I wrote off the computer company, my current coworkers, and any prospects within the existing job. I decided to do no more and no less than I had to in order to collect my paycheck. I spent my every creative moment on a surreptitious job search.

Six months later, I was still searching. And still writing, "Insert any three-digit figure." I was becoming increasingly frustrated. Surely, the Lord had better things in mind for me than this! Angrily, I put in my seven and a quarter hours and spent every other available moment scanning the "Help Wanted" ads.

At the end of the eighth month, I was desperate. My boredom with the job was almost intolerable, and there was no immediate relief in sight. I decided that I was stuck, and I might as well get used to the idea.

I started to make some friends among my co-workers. I volunteered for some extra assignments. I took my eyes off the "Help Wanted" columns and started reading the "Computer Business" pages. Much to my surprise, I began to enjoy the work.

When one of my new friends mentioned that the sales department needed some marketing help, I offered to put together a program for them. From there, I found myself being asked to take on all kinds of tasks in other areas of interest. I taught some software courses, designed advertising campaigns, went on sales calls, and put together marketing studies.

Shortly after that, I applied for a job that was everything I had ever wanted to do. I got the dream job, but only because of the extra things I had done in the past year.

I had been where the Lord wanted me all along. But I had wasted so much time longing to be somewhere else.

———————————

I don't like blooming where I'm planted. I'm always convinced that I will be a more exciting blossom somewhere else, preferably some place of my own choosing. I spend a lot of time holding back on my blooms until something better comes along. Of course, holding back on anything leads to frustration, and as I grow more frustrated in my situation, I hold back even more. It is a vicious, self-defeating cycle.

I am always sure that I am destined for far greater things, far more important things, than the people around me. Deep inside, I am sure that a terrible mistake has been made, and just as soon as Somebody realizes the error, I'll be transplanted to a situation where my blooms will be appreciated. In the meantime, I'll keep them to myself.

I have withheld my blooms in so many areas of my life.

In jobs I have perceived as dead-end or boring, I have bided my time, waiting, waiting, either for a new job or for my pension, whichever comes along first.

In relationships, I have held back, waiting, waiting, for the ''right'' person to give my love to.

In my church, I have sat in my comfortable pew, waiting, waiting, for God to send a new, dynamic pastor or at least a committed, exciting congregation.

I wait for God to *do something* while I do nothing but wait. I hold myself back and wonder why I feel trapped and useless.

TEN

Diet Is a Four-letter Word

But God keeps his promise, and he will not allow you to be tested beyond your power to remain firm; at the time you are put to the test, he will give you the strength to endure it, and so provide you with a way out.

—1 Corinthians 10:13

TEN

Moments of truth are never fun! They're never convenient, either.

One such moment of truth struck me when I was getting ready to take a business trip to a convention in Houston. As usual, I'd left my packing to the last minute, not because I was particularly rushed, but because my business wardrobe is always ready to hit the road at a moment's notice. The standard gray suit, the white silk blouse, several bright scarves, two pairs of shoes, and the string of pearls to dress the whole shebang up for the evening. If I was going to be away for more than two days, I threw in the navy suit, the pink blouse, and a gold chain or two. No problem.

Then I read the fine print on the convention program. I hadn't realized that Houston meant cowboys, and cowboys meant that every evening's program was geared to the wild west, the outdoors, the home-on-the-range feeling. The fine print said: "Dress—western gear." I thought furiously. Western gear . . . boots (check!), plaid shirt (check!), bandanna (check!), and jeans. Jeans? Where were my jeans? It had been some time since I'd worn them. Somehow, I'd gotten into the habit of slipping into jogging pants when I wanted to go casual. "So much more comfortable," I told myself, "after a week strapped into panty hose and skirts."

I unearthed my jeans from the back of my closet. They looked fine. Zipper worked, knees and seat still intact, no gaping seams. Just to be on the safe side, I decided to quickly try them on.

That was the moment of truth I was telling you about. Those jeans must have shrunk two sizes while they lay in the back of the closet, probably out of spite because I wasn't wearing them anymore.

There was no way—either by sucking in my stomach or by lying flat on my back—that I was ever going to do up the zipper. Even if I were to limit my food to celery sticks and ice water for the next two days (or the next six weeks), those jeans still wouldn't fit.

It had happened again! Ounce by ounce, inch by inch, I had slowly edged to my present state of elephant! There was nothing to do but wear my most western-looking jogging pants to the party! I didn't win any rave reviews from the fashion critics at the convention.

Sometimes I get tired of the never-ending struggle to keep in shape, or at least in a shape that will fit my current wardrobe. I don't remember having to be so vigilant when I was younger. In fact, I can remember a time in the not-too-distant past when I could have a double fudge sundae without waking up to find it on my hips the next morning.

Not so these days. These days it's a constant battle of the bulge. *Diet* has become a four-letter word.

There are few people in the Western world who haven't at one time or another been on a diet. Even the little skinny types diet to grow fatter... their diet is just the opposite of what the rest of us worry about, but it is a diet all the same. Dieting is an art of self-control that few people master. A quick glance around makes this abundantly clear. Diet workshops, diet centers, diet foods, diet clinics, diet therapy, diet conferences, diet weekends, diet spas—they all give us the same message. We cannot control what goes into our little rosebud mouths!

How silly! Such a small degree of control is needed. Simply say no, push away from the table, keep my mouth shut or, as a last resort, don't swallow. What's the problem?

The problem is that dieting is more than a matter of knowing what to do. I know what I should eat; I know to the last calorie exactly how much is required to sustain me; I know the nutritional content of virtually every food on the grocery shelves. Yet, when push comes to shove, the old bodily desires win out every time.

Anyone who has ever fought the battle of the bulge

knows how difficult it is to overcome temptation in the form of that second piece of pie, that handful of potato chips, or that last helping of mashed potatoes, which is really too small to be saved for another day. Anyway, isn't it a sin to waste good food when there are so many hungry people in the world?

When I am on a diet, I feel like an army in a constant state of siege. At any moment, my defenses can be breached by the stray aroma of freshly baked bread, the sight of a chocolate bar in a child's hand, or the sound of the ice-cream truck. Food assails me from every direction, and only constant vigilance prevents me from complete surrender. Golden arches, revolving red-and-white buckets, flashing neon cones, little dough boys, bananas wearing rhumba skirts, dancing hot dogs, talking pickles— all mount a frontal attack on my weakening willpower. *Overcoming temptation* is a polite term for war.

I wish I could say that it was a war I always won or even a battle in which I could count on being the victor. However, such is not the case. I'm writing this "thin," but chances are by the time you read this, I won't be anymore. Thin, that is. I'm good for a year, and then the pendulum swings, the yo-yo returns, the ball bounces back, and the fat returns. Each time, it gets a little harder to get rid of, and I have a dread that the time will finally come when the double chins and the spare tire are here to stay.

Perhaps it is just as well if they are. They serve as constant reminders to me that I'm not as strong as I would like to think I am.

————————

Whenever I begin to think that I can overcome the temptation to sin in my life, I just remember dieting. Funny, I cheerfully admit to all and sundry that I have a problem staying on a diet, but I hate to admit that there might be the slightest problem with sin in my life. After all, I don't consider myself in the "Big S" class of Sinners—like thieves and murderers and the like.

Sin is such a big word to describe the things I have to fight: little white lies, small larcenies, petty thefts, and minor slanders. Just a little over the speed limit; only a few pencils from the office; a little padding on a business resume; a juicy tidbit of gossip about the lady across the street.

All small sins—hardly worth worrying about. Except, like that extra piece of cake, that second helping of mashed potatoes, those small sins add up, too, and lead to much worse consequences than double chins and spare tires.

However, I have the winning edge in this spiritual battle. I know that the spirit of God is on my side. Whenever I feel myself tempted to allow even the smallest sin to enter my life, I remind myself that God has promised that I will not be tested beyond my power to remain firm. If all else fails, God has even promised me the strength I need to endure.

If only a diet could make that kind of promise!

Looking for Birds of a Feather

Let us not give up the habit of meeting together, as some are doing. Instead, let us encourage one another all the more, since you see that the Day of the Lord is coming nearer.

—Hebrews 10:25

ELEVEN

The other day I happened to mention that I knew a nearby small community because "I go to church there." The reactions to that simple statement were astounding:

"You're just trying to impress us by telling us you go to church."

"Boy, I never thought that you were one of those religious fanatics."

"Sure you do. Next you'll be telling us that you go every Sunday."

"Are you trying to make me feel guilty or something?"

"Going to church" has become an endangered activity, and few people will openly admit to participating in such a dubious practice. Church is for children to go to Sunday school, and for old folks who think they're getting close to their "Final Exam," I've been told. Regular people don't need church except, of course, for weddings, baptisms, and funerals. And maybe at Easter, just to keep Grandma happy.

That's all presuming that you have a church home to use on those few occasions when it's needed. Finding a church home is just about as difficult as admitting that you need one in the first place!

Shortly after I was divorced, I decided that I should seek a new church in order to prevent embarrassment for the congregation that didn't know which party to invite to the Annual Dinner.

It had been some years since I had gone to a church as anything other than the minister's wife, and I was more than a little nervous about venturing into "foreign" territory. At the time, I had two preschoolers, so it was vital that I find a church with a good Sunday school. I like to sing, so I hoped for one with an active choir. Most importantly, I needed a church that would love and accept me in a time when I most needed fellowship.

My shopping list also included an evangelical pastor, an active prayer group, Bible study sessions, and a convenient location. I realized that I wouldn't find all that I wanted, but I was willing to settle for as close to perfection as possible.

While I was still perusing the church page in the local newspaper and trying to convince myself that the services on television were just as good as the real thing, my friend Diane suggested that I'd like to come along to church with her.

At last! Something tangible that came with its own endorsement. I knew that Diane was Episcopalian, but I also had been many years earlier. I would feel right at home in the service. I knew that the church was a larger, downtown establishment, and I hoped that that would guarantee an equally large Sunday school. I knew that the choir often sang in other churches, so I presumed that the level of musical ability would be fairly high.

On a cold, snowy Sunday morning we arrived for the eleven o'clock service. We were running late, so I rushed the children downstairs to the Sunday school room. Nathan bluntly refused to be left in the nursery. He was sticking with Mommy in this strange building. Cherith took one look at the rocking horses and settled down happily.

Nathan and I met Diane upstairs, and she led us to her regular pew, about two rows from the front. I would have preferred a less conspicuous position, say in the back corner by the door, behind a pillar or two, but I had little choice. I tried to explain to Nathan what the little benches on the floor were for. He wanted to sit on one, but I managed to convince him they were just for kneeling. He wanted to know why he didn't have one at home by the bed.

The service began with a processional down the aisle. I had forgotten that Diane's church was considered of the "high" persuasion. Nathan wanted to know why the man was wearing a dress. I explained it was a special costume just for church.

The service moved on smoothly, and I began to enjoy

the feeling of coming home as the familiar phrases from the *Prayer Book* filled the church. When the minister mounted the pulpit to begin his sermon, I sat back in eager expectation.

He spoke on the family. Or more to the point, he spoke on the importance of the family in today's world and went on to speak against divorce. It hurt, hearing words condemning me, especially when I was feeling insecure and unhappy in my single state. I wanted to jump up and tell him that life wasn't as black and white as he was painting it. I felt my eyes fill with tears, and to my horror, they spilled over onto my cheeks. Surreptitiously, I tried to wipe them away. Nathan, who never misses anything, said loudly, "Why are you crying, Mommy?" I tried to hush him. He wasn't about to be hushed. He was, by this time, bored and tired of the novelty of a new church. He decided to push the point. "Where's my daddy? Is he still in his church?"

I decided it was time to beat a hasty retreat. I gathered up my things and took Nathan's arm. As quietly as possible, I started up the long center aisle, head down, anxious to get out. Nathan decided that things were just getting interesting.

"Why are we going, Mommy? Ow! Don't grab my arm! You're pinching me, Mommy! Ow! Ow! You're hurting me!"

We had the undivided attention of the entire congregation for our complete retreat up the aisle.

They also continued to listen as I headed downstairs for the Sunday school room to pick up Cherith.

"Why are we going, Mommy? Are you still crying? Are we going to see Daddy? Ow! Don't hold my arm! I don't want to go!"

I never went back again.

But I learned that one vital tip to remember on your first visit to a new church is to think inconspicuous. Leave the children with a baby-sitter, dress conservatively, be on time, and sit near the back.

Anyone else would have given up after an experience like that, but I kept looking for a church home. I recognized that my loneliness stemmed from lack of fellowship, and that by cutting myself off from the body of Christ, I was condemning myself to a lonely, solitary existence that no secular club or group could change. I realized that we Christians need to meet together regularly. We need to be in touch with the body of Christ, to be fed spiritual food on a regular basis, to be part of the larger family.

I kept looking for a church, and I eventually found one where I felt welcomed and comfortable. The Sunday school was small, the choir dwindling in numbers, but the church members went out of their way to help me find a place in their congregation.

When I meet people who tell me that they never bother going to church because they can commune with God just as easily on a Sunday morning walk in the woods, I remind them that we do not go to church to commune with God once a week. We can do that anytime. We go to church to meet with our fellow Christians, to share the burdens and joys of our lives, and to encourage one another on the journey ahead of us.

Has Anybody Seen My Mary?

Each one should judge his own conduct. If it is good, then he can be proud of what he himself has done, without having to compare it with what someone else has done. For everyone has to carry his own load.

—Galatians 6:4-5

TWELVE

I've decided that I need some "Mary" lessons.

Remember the biblical story about Martha and Mary? Jesus was visiting at their house, and after the meal, Martha went to the kitchen to do the dishes. Mary stayed in the parlor and visited with Jesus. Martha was angry that she ended up doing all the work while Mary had all the fun.

Two thousand years later, women still seem to fall naturally into two groups: there are the Marthas, and there are the Marys. I used to think that all it took was a meal of any kind to immediately identify them. The Marthas are the ones who automatically stack the dishes and head for the kitchen. If it's not their kitchen they're heading for, they tell you that they'll come and "fellowship" with you over the dishes.

Please don't offer to come and fellowship over the dishes with me. I'd rather leave the whole pile and hope the dish-fairy will come before I get up in the morning.

I don't want to help out in a strange kitchen, either. I

don't like trying to figure out where the soup ladle goes and how to pass the quality control inspection of the resident Martha.

I've always put down my unconcern with washing the dishes to what I thought was my natural Mary nature. Actually, I just don't like doing dishes, and I'm beginning to realize that all these years I've been a Martha in disguise.

For example, Marthas can't walk away and leave the dishes until morning. Deep inside, they're convinced that if they let those dishes wait, this will be the time they are carted off to the hospital for some emergency or other, and when their friends come back to the house to pick up a few items for them, the first thing they'll see is the unwashed dishes! It will be only a matter of hours before Martha's entire social circle will know that she is the kind of person who leaves dirty dishes in the sink.

You may smile at the picture. I did, until I remembered the time I found out that I had to go to the hospital for some fairly major surgery. I had three days' notice. Did I spend it making out a will? No. Visiting my friends? No. Spending time with my family? No.

This Martha spent the time before her hospital stay cleaning, cleaning, cleaning. I even washed, ironed, and *starched* every tablecloth and napkin I owned. "If I should die before I wake," heaven forbid that anyone ever see how I really live! (There are some days when I almost wish for just another such emergency. We've never been that clean since then.)

I also like to think that Marthas spend endless hours in the kitchen preparing meals for their ungrateful loved ones. I class myself as a Mary because my family is intimately familiar with macaroni and cheese, Hamburger Helper, and Twinkies. A Martha's teenager has never come home from school to a mother who says, "D.I.Y. tonight." (D.I.Y. stands for Do It Yourself, which means if you can find it, cook it, and eat it, consider it supper.)

Hah! The true Martha hidden deep inside me has other ways to let her family know how much she sacrifices to make them happy. "What do you mean you're not hungry after I hurried home from work with a splitting headache just to cook this special dish for you?" That usually guarantees a certain degree of gratitude. Or "Of course I'll stay up half the night baking cookies for your class. I don't mind. It's no bother, really." Followed by a deep sigh and a yawn, this one's a surefire guilt builder.

You see, Marthas are martyrs. Unfortunately, it's not a silent martyrdom.

One summer in Newfoundland, an envangelical singing group stayed with us on their tour. I cooked and cleaned and did dishes. By the end of the third day, I was in "full martyrdom"—I sighed, I rolled my eyes, I looked pitiful. At every opportunity, I reminded my husband how wonderful I was to be doing all the work so that he and the group could enjoy themselves.

I had made it halfway through a sinkful of dishes one evening; suddenly, the gang barged into the kitchen and offered to help me. "No, no," I protested. "I'll do them. It's no bother, really. You go on into the living room and enjoy yourselves." Sigh. Roll eyes heavenward.

They didn't buy it. They bodily picked me up and carried me out of the kitchen. Then they declared the sink off-limits to me! I realized how silly I had been not to let them help from the first day or, alternatively, to do the work willingly myself as part of my contribution to the success of their tour (and ultimately to the Lord's work).

All these years, I've thought that I was a Mary because I didn't worry about things like dust bunnies under the bed, spotted glasses in the dishwasher, or whether my towels were soft and fluffy. And all the time, I was really a Martha. I needed the Mary lessons.

Otherwise, I might become one of those middle-aged, bitter Marthas who make everyone around them feel guilty for enjoying life.

If you read further into the account of Mary and Martha, you'll realize that Jesus wasn't angry with Martha for doing the dishes. He was angry with her because she was crying, "Poor me." Doing the dishes was her own choice. She could just as easily have chosen to join Mary at Jesus' feet.

The Mary lessons tell me that life is to be lived in a way that gives other people the freedom to be Marys if they choose to be.

I'm also learning that Martha's heavy burden can become Mary's joyful service. It's up to me.

Down in the Garden Eating Worms

I may have all knowledge and understand all secrets; I may have all the faith needed to move mountains—but if I have no love, I am nothing.

—1 Corinthians 13:2

THIRTEEN

Nobody loves me, everybody hates me,
Going down to the garden to eat worms. . . .

My teenagers seem to spend most of their adolescent years down in the garden eating worms. It's as if they have a built-in sense of being unloved. From the moment puberty strikes until sometime after their eighteenth birthday, young people are convinced that they are unlovable creatures.

When I watch either Nathan or Cherith assessing his/her physical features in a mirror, it's no wonder he/she feels unlovable. The nose is too long; the hair is too thick; the eyes are too small. He/she is too short, too tall, too thin, too fat. "My legs are funny"; "my ears don't match"; "my knees are ugly."

I'm amazed that either of them ever gets out the door and allows the rest of the world to see such a blemished human being!

Not only do they consider their appearance a strike

against them in this world, they are also convinced that nobody out there understands them. Teachers don't, neighbors don't, and I certainly don't. Their only allies are their friends, and even these relationships are rocky at best. This week's companion for life is next week's world's worst enemy.

In the midst of this turmoil, I, poor parent, try my best to let them know that they are loved just as they are. But they want none of it. They won't accept any display of affection ("Don't hug me—I'm not a kid anymore") or emotional interest ("You're always bugging me about what I'm feeling") or material gifts ("But I wanted *blue* ones").

Most of my bumbling overtures of love are met with a slammed door followed by muffled rock music. They are happy in their world of self-condemnation, and they'd like to keep it that way. "Go away" has become a familiar refrain.

Until, one day, something happens. I'm not sure what, but suddenly, they are willing to be loved again. Cherith kisses me hello, Nathan tells me his troubles, and both thank me for my latest offering.

Now that I'm grown up, I don't have the disease of "teenagitis" to blame for my feelings of being unloved, but I have moments when I might as well be fifteen years old. I can remember a time when I was down in the garden eating worms and didn't even realize it.

Shortly after I moved to Toronto, I was invited to take part in a weekend conference in Vancouver. This was a very great honor for me, and I was excited about the prospect of sharing the weekend with George Anderson, the Canadian director of Faith at Work. We flew to Vancouver together and were met by some friends who whisked us away to their home for a preconference planning meeting. I enjoyed being one of the consultants who had been brought in for the occasion, and I especially enjoyed the extra attention it brought me. I felt important, special, and needed.

The conference had come at a time when I was still in the throes of putting my life back together. I was a little shaky about living as a single parent, being the sole support of a family, and worrying about things like mortgages and heating bills. I hadn't had time to assess how I was actually feeling about the whole business; I was simply living through each day as it came. I hoped that the conference would give me an opportunity to do some soul-searching and an opportunity to ask the Lord to fill in the missing pieces in my life.

On the morning of the opening sessions, our host drove us to the church, which was about twenty miles from their home. George and I sat in the backseat, both unusually silent for two naturally gregarious people. No doubt George was immersed in thoughts about the upcoming morning. I was desperately trying to recover from jet lag.

Suddenly, I felt the back of George's hand stroke my cheek. I looked up in surprise. "I just wanted to say that

I'm glad you're here with me. We love you.'' He smiled and turned back to his own thoughts.

I was dumbfounded and completely unnerved. I can still feel the emotions of that moment. Shock. Joy. Love. You see, it had been a long time since someone had touched me lovingly, or since I had touched anyone else. I mean *touch,* not just in the physical manifestation, but in the best sense of the word. George's simple gesture had touched me deeply, and I suddenly realized what had been happening to me. I had allowed myself to become unloved. Love was the missing piece in my current life.

After that moment, I went out of my way to let others know that I loved them. I touched them—with words, with gestures, with actions. It was as if I had opened the floodgates. I was loved in return.

Love is a reciprocal affair. I can be loved only if I allow myself to be. When the phone doesn't ring, it's up to me to make the call. When a hug doesn't happen, I need to make the first move. When I feel unloved, I need to love first.

It's the same way with God's love. The Lord can love me until the cows come home, but unless I allow that wonderful love to touch me, I'll continue to feel unloved.

I need to remind myself that God's love is always waiting for me because it gets lonely down in the garden eating worms.

FOURTEEN

Be Reasonable —Do It My Way

Be always humble, gentle, and patient. Show your love by being tolerant with one another. Do your best to preserve the unity which the Spirit gives by means of the peace that binds you together.

—Ephesians 4:2-3

FOURTEEN

People keep telling me that I will need less and less sleep as I grow older. They tell me that I can expect to begin waking earlier and earlier in the day, and in no time at all, I'll become a veritable morning person. This is not a pleasant thought for me.

You see, I can probably count on the fingers of one hand the number of sunrises I've voluntarily witnessed.

I tend to agree with the person who said that if God had meant us to see the sun rise, God would have scheduled it for later in the day. It's not that I'm against sunrises; it's just that this whole morning business has gotten entirely out of hand. I'm tired of the "early bird," and I suspect that he is probably tired of worms. I don't want to be healthy, wealthy, and wise. I'll take my chances with my body, bankbook, and brains and settle for that extra hour's sleep.

That is, if I could get it.

I am constantly deterred from it by those so-called morning people whose biological alarm clock is divinely set to go off at 5:00 A.M. (daylight saving and standard time included) and who bound out of bed eager to face the day ahead. They are the ones who always call me at 7:00 on Saturday morning ("Oh, did I wake you? Goodness, I've been up for hours"—all the while I'm thinking, *Bully for you*) and ask me if I would bring two dozen cookies to next Wednesday's ladies' Bible study. They know that my "no" power is proportionally diminished by the earliness of the hour, and I'll agree to anything.

These morning people are also the ones who schedule breakfast meetings. "Smorgasbord breakfast at 7:00, followed by a stimulating group discussion." They must be kidding. In order to be up, dressed, and in my right mind, I'd have to start somewhere around 4:00 A.M. Frankly, I doubt that anything can be stimulating after juice, bacon, eggs, muffins, flapjacks, and sausages. My entire body is too concerned with the digestion of this bonanza to waste any effort or oxygen on mere brain cells. (Does the early bird enjoy a stimulating postworm discussion, I wonder?)

Inevitably, it is a morning person, one who jogs three miles before her high-protein ("wheat germ and raw eggs, so good for the complexion") blender breakfast, who feels honor-bound to tell me what is happening to my caffeine-starved system as I reach for my midmorning cup.

I really don't want to know. If they must extol the virtues of early rising, couldn't they do it a little later in the day? Say, around midnight, when my adrenaline is finally pumping, when my gears have shifted into high, and I am ready (nay, eager) to tackle the monumental task of cleaning the shower.

At midnight, however, I'm safe from those morning people. They have long since packed it in and are resting their bodies in preparation for a high-powered dawn start.

That's when I'd like to call my morning friend and tell her about my new cookie recipe or perhaps get the gang together for a late supper and consciousness-raising session.

I'd just as soon have everyone become a night owl like me. In fact, I'm going to start spreading the rumor that aging causes people to sleep later and later in the morning, and go to bed later and later at night.

Midnight bingo, anyone?

How boring it would be if we were all the same! And how wonderful it was of the Lord to make us all in our diversity! Now, if only I could learn to accept and enjoy the ways in which other Christians aren't like me.

Then I'd probably rejoice with my brothers and sisters who like to raise the church roof with a few "hallelujahs" now and then. Or I'd feel equally comfortable with those fellow travelers who sit in silence and meditate before the Lord. I might join in with a rousing gospel-playing brass band or participate in a solemn age-old ritual.

Instead, I feel the same way about the differences of my fellow Christians as I feel about those people who don't even get up when I do. I want to change them, make them like me, or at least shut them out and ignore them.

Maybe I should check out a sunrise or two. Who knows what I might be missing?

Who's in the Driver's Seat?

Those who live as their human nature tells them to, have their minds controlled by what human nature wants. Those who live as the Spirit tells them to, have their minds controlled by what the Spirit wants.

—Romans 8:5

FIFTEEN

Sometimes I get the feeling that my life is running me and not the other way around. The feeling is usually strongest on those days when no matter how you slice it, there just isn't enough time (or enough *me*) to satisfy everything and everybody. Those are the days when the old adage about "running around like chickens with their heads cut off" takes on a new significance.

I used to have a lot of days like that. At the end of one of them, I'd collapse into bed, too tired to even question why I was too tired to question why! The next morning I'd hit the deck running, and it would start all over again. I began to feel as if I had stepped onto some kind of cosmic treadmill.

Usually, it took a bout of sickness to stop me. My poor, beleaguered body would holler "Halt!" and I'd spend a day or two in bed, just long enough to recover my strength. Of course, by the time I returned to the combat zone, sixty-three new things had been added to the already growing list of things to do, people to see, and places to visit—or more prosaically, groceries to get, teachers to discuss with, and dentists to be at.

I couldn't figure out why I seemed doomed to a lifestyle that left very little time for Patricia and even less time for the rest. Somewhere, somehow, something had gone terribly wrong, but I didn't have time to find out what.

At the most hectic point in my life, my boss decided that it was my turn to take some professional development courses. "Pick a course that's in a nice location," he advised. "Some of them run for several days, and if you choose a course that's held in one of the resort areas, you'll have a mini-vacation as well." *Sound advice,* I thought as I perused the list of courses available to me. Finally, I chose "Stress Management," not because I was under any particular stress, but because it was held at a popular resort inn, and it lasted three days.

I wasn't sure if I could really afford three days off my treadmill, but I figured if I baked and cooked and planned and stockpiled, everyone would be able to manage without the manager around. On the surface, I complained about being sent on silly courses when I was so busy, but inside, I was looking forward to three days of rest and recreation. And oh yes, with a little bit of stress management thrown in—but only to justify my expenses.

I arrived at the inn late on Sunday evening. Within minutes, I realized that I had made a very wise choice indeed. My room had a fireplace, large-screen television, whirlpool bath, and gourmet room-service menu. Could I ask for anything more? It seemed a shame that the course was going to cut into my well-planned leisure time, but with luck, I hoped to be able to keep the interruptions to a minimum.

Monday morning, twenty of us assembled in the designated meeting room. We were an interesting assortment of people from various departments of a large provincial civil service. After the standard introductions, the leader asked us to share our reasons for coming to this particular course. Some of the group talked about their own stress areas; others admitted that they feared they were heading for burnout. One man even wept as he talked about the breakup of his marriage and his inability to cope with the new stresses in his life.

I wasn't sure I wanted to tell them that I had decided I'd like a three-day holiday at a well-known resort inn. So, I explained that I didn't feel that I was under any particular stress, but hoped I'd benefit in some way from the course.

Then we were given a stress evaluation test to do: a thick comprehensive document of hundreds of unrelated questions, such as "I would rather do it myself than let someone else do a poor job of it," and "There's never enough time in the day to get everything done," and "People expect me to create their good times and good feelings." It ended with a complicated scoring procedure.

113

I added up my score. Checked it. Checked it again. Asked the instructor to clarify the scoring system. Added it up again. Asked the instructor to check that I was doing it right. I was.

I had the highest score in the group. If all the indicators were correct, I was on the verge of a glorious stress burnout. Me. Mrs. Wonderful Wife, Mother, Homemaker, Career Woman, Professonal Writer, Public Speaker, Chauffeur, Chief Cook and Bottle Washer. I was sure there was some mistake.

I secretly wondered if the stress test were rigged so that group members would feel obliged to stick with the course, despite the siren calls of their fireplace and whirlpool bath. A surreptitious check around the room dispelled the notion. There were people in the group who weren't in the least bit stressed. They had probably just come for a freeloading vacation at a resort inn!

Needless to say, after the rude awakening to my stressful state. I hung on every word the instructor said. The ashes in my fireplace grew cold, and I never even figured out how to turn on the whirlpool in my tub. But I did find out what was causing my stress or, to be more exact, what was ''driving'' me.

One of the concepts we examined in the course was that of Drivers. These are nasty little external messages that we learn from others (usually notables in our lives like parents, teachers, and siblings) or that we push onto ourselves. They are called Drivers because they do just that: drive us harder and harder until we collapse under their relentless pressure.

There is a Driver called "Hurry Up." Like the White Rabbit in *Alice's Adventures in Wonderland,* people driven by "Hurry Up" have no time for anything. In fact, time is seen as an enemy that must be beaten. Their lives are spent rushing from one project to another, and in their drive to accomplish more and do more, they take on more responsibilities and are driven even harder.

Then there's the Driver called "Be Perfect." This Driver tells its victims that things must always be perfect, that less-than-perfect is never acceptable, and that making mistakes of any kind is wrong. "Be perfect"–driven people continually grade themselves and refuse to accept anything less than 100 percent.

Many are caught by the "Please Others" Driver. They feel that they are responsible for other people's happiness and good feelings. They feel worthwhile only if they are doing things for other people, regardless of their own needs. But they get depressed if their own needs aren't met, and they expect others to know what those needs are without being told. They need to be liked by everyone and have never learned to say no.

The "Be Strong" Driver prevents people from participating in open and honest relationships. It will not allow any kind of "weak" emotions and cannot accept vulnerability in any form. Often, the "Be Strong" Driver covers up with a show of anger and never, never, allows its victim to ask for help. These people feel OK only when they are strong and tough.

And finally, there is the "Try Harder" Driver. People driven by this know that nothing of value comes easily and that life is one long, unending struggle. They feel like victims fighting against overwhelming odds. They know that work is not supposed to be pleasurable, and results can be measured only by the amount of effort expended.

By the time we had come to the end of the Drivers, I could see where my pressures were coming from. I was caught by "Hurry Up" and "Please Others." I was married to a "Be Perfect." I had a difficult employee who carried the "Try Harder" banner. No wonder I was nearly off the stress scale.

But, we were told, on the other side of these Drivers are Permitters. These Permitters are internally generated. They are the freedom fighters in our lives. They give us permission to go at our own pace, please ourselves, be open and vulnerable, enjoy success without trying too hard, and make mistakes once in a while.

The goal of the stress management course was to get us in touch with our Permitters. Then, freed from the pressure of our Drivers and able to understand our reactions to others people's Drivers, we would lead less stressful lives.

I had an advantage over the rest of the group. I personally knew the Divine Permitter. I had already been promised a life more abundant: the life of a Permitted Person. Once I understood that it wasn't the Lord who was insisting that I hurry up, or try hard, or please others, or be strong, or be perfect, but an external driver that I had allowed to take control of my life, I was free to be Permitted.

Now, if I please others, it's from a desire to please, not from guilt; and if I'm hurrying to do something, it's because it's my natural pace that I don't have to inflict on others. I can understand those who need to try hard, and I can be patient with their dogged efforts. And if I run into the "Be Perfect" Driver of my husband, I no longer resent his insistence that we do it right, not fast, the first time.

More important, now when I feel as if my life is running me again, I stop and ask myself, "Who's in the driver's seat?"

SIXTEEN

Nobody Likes a Party Pooper!

The Spirit that God has given us does not make us timid; instead, his Spirit fills us with power, love, and self-control.

—*2 Timothy 1:7*

SIXTEEN

They told me it was a good idea. Sitting in Helga's kitchen, enjoying a sample of her fresh goat's milk and cheese, both Nathan and Gerald assured me that they really liked the taste.

"Would you put it on your cereal?" I asked suspiciously, thinking of the endless gallons of milk used in our household for just this purpose.

"Oh yes," they both chorused. "You can't tell the difference from regular milk."

"Come out to the barn and meet Nanny," said Helga, who no doubt sensed victory within her grasp.

We followed her out to the goat pens and met Nanny, a white Saanen goat of uncertain years. She looked about as unimpressed with us as I felt about her. Helga gave us a quick milking demonstration. It looked easy.

It was time for me to say no. I could see that both Gerald and Nathan were a little uneasy about the idea of actually milking Nanny, and in my heart of hearts I knew that neither of them had really thought about this aspect of the operation. They were just looking at a never-ending supply of milk.

I also knew that they wouldn't like having to be tied down to a daily milking routine. The question of where we would actually put Nanny was another good reason to say no.

But I didn't. I didn't want to spoil their fun. I didn't want to be the wet blanket, the negative noodle, the party pooper. I kept silent. Well, not really. I distanced myself from the whole business.

"Remember," I said sternly, "I'm not having anything to do with this goat. I don't mind chickens, and I don't mind donkeys, but I don't like goats, and they don't like me. If we take Nanny, you fellows are in charge."

Gerald and Nathan agreed readily, visions of gallons of fresh milk no doubt dancing in their heads. Gerald asked Helga some questions about feeding and milking and general care. I tuned out. It wasn't my concern.

"I'll bring her around tomorrow morning," said Helga as we left. She was off on a global trip and was glad to have found a good home for Nanny.

The next morning, Helga arrived with both Nanny and her milking stand in the back of the station wagon. Gerald brought his new milk producer up to the barn and turned her into the donkey pasture. He had decided that the donkeys would be pleased to share their stall and pasture with one small white lady goat.

He was dead wrong. Lexy took one look at Nanny and

saw a rival for her family's attention and affection. Head down, she chased Nanny across the field. It was obvious that we were going to end up with goat's butter instead of milk if we didn't rescue Nanny. Gerald grudgingly rigged up a pen in the corner of the barn where the donkeys couldn't get at her.

Soon, it was evening. Milking time. I stayed in the house. Gerald and Nathan set off optimistically for the barn. Twenty minutes later, Nathan returned to ask if I could give them a hand. I reminded him that I didn't want to have anything to do with the goat.

"Go and ask Janet across the road. She's milked cows and things. Goats are probably the same." A few minutes later, I saw Janet heading for our barn.

An hour later, Gerald and Nathan returned to the house. They were hot, dirty, and disheveled. They were also empty-handed.

"Where's the goat's milk?" I asked them.

"She kicked over the bucket," growled Gerald. I didn't think that I should press for details.

Morning came. Milking time again.

"Could you give us a hand?" Gerald looked pleadingly at me. "Janet's not around today, and I haven't quite got it worked out yet."

I couldn't say no. This was one of those "for better or for worse" situations.

At the barn, Nathan coaxed Nanny onto her milking stand. He filled a bucket with oats, and Nanny stuck her head through the neck stock and started to eat. Gerald positoned the bucket. The moment he touched her, Nanny sat down.

You can do a lot of things in this world in impossible situations, but you cannot milk a goat who is sitting down.

Gerald lifted up her back end and repositioned the bucket. Nanny pulled her head free from the stock, glared balefully at Gerald, and neatly kicked the bucket over.

Nathan got her head back between the restraining bars.

"Hold her head in there," commanded Gerald, once again positioning the bucket. He reached under her nether regions. Nanny sat down, knocking over the bucket.

Gerald lifted her up. She sat down.

"I'll hold her up. You milk her," he said to me.

"What! Me? I've never milked anything in my life!" And I certainly didn't intend to start at my age. I didn't like the idea of sticking my hands under a goat and touching parts that were, in my opinion, better left untouched.

"Well, you can't lift her," he said with an uncharacteristic edge of anger in his voice. "She's too heavy. Let's just get this over with."

We milked Nanny. Nathan stood at her head and held her horns. Gerald straddled her middle, facing backward, and lifted up her whole back end. I got underneath and did what had to be done. It took just over an hour.

When we were finished and Nanny had all fours back on terra firma, she looked at Gerald and kicked over the bucket of milk.

"Call Helga," he said. "Tell her to come and get her goat."

"You call her," I retorted. "Nanny was your idea. I don't even like milk."

I made us all a cup of coffee (without goat's milk) while Gerald phoned. He looked like a thundercloud when he returned.

"She can't take Nanny back. She's leaving in the morning for Indonesia, and there'll be no one at the farm to take care of Nanny."

We looked at one another. Nanny was about to become a member of our family. It was now late morning. Soon it would be afternoon, and then evening, and milking time again. And again. And again.

"Let's go for a drive this afternoon," I said. "We'll worry about the milking later." Gratefully, we escaped the world of Nanny.

When we returned home, Gerald offered to make some lemonade. Nathan went up to the barn to see how Nanny was faring. He came tearing back to the house.

"She's gone! Nanny's gone! Her milking stand is there, but her pen's open. I think she's run away!"

Gerald unconcernedly continued to make the lemonade.

"What are we going to do?" continued Nathan. "She's probably run off into the back forty."

Gerald put the drinks on a tray and carried them out to the patio.

"She'll be lost if she gets into the cedar trees!"

Gerald picked a glass and settled back into his favorite lawn chair.

"Aren't you going to look for her?" asked Nathan.

"Later, later." Gerald took a long sip. "There's no hurry. When she gets hungry. She'll come home." Nanny had no knight in shining armor here who was going to come to her rescue. I suspect that he rather hoped that Nanny would never come home. It was getting on for "that" time of the day again.

Just then, the phone rang. It was Helga. She had found a home for Nanny, had come by and picked her up, and would get the milking stand some other time.

Nanny had been with us for just twenty-four hours.

I didn't say, "I told you so," because I hadn't. I hadn't honestly told Gerald and Nathan how I felt about Nanny, even though I knew that a goat wasn't a good idea, given the fact that none of us had any real "goat experience." I didn't want to spoil their party. To mix metaphors, I had "washed my hands of the whole affair" and let them have "enough rope to hang themselves." Not very loving. Not very brave.

In retrospect, I didn't do the boys, or Nanny, any favors. I ended up feeling guilty and uncomfortable and not at all as smug as I thought I would be. "I told you so'' would have had a hollow ring from someone who was too afraid to risk the unpopularity of a party pooper!

It's hard to be a party pooper! Being a Christian, and a parent, oftens means that I'm seen as an all-enveloping wet blanket on any number of great schemes that my children are invited to participate in.

Often, it's hard to explain exactly why I'm saying no. On the surface, the idea (such as a sleep-over at an unknown friend's house) seems harmless. Yet, some inner sense warns me that danger lies ahead.

I hesitate. Should I say no, based on the what I hope is the gentle nudge of the Spirit? This is so difficult to explain to a fifteen-year-old with visions of good times in his head. Or should I play the role of Fun Mom and let him join in with the gang, telling myself that I can rely on his fifteen-year-old good judgment?

Then, I remember our twenty-four-hour goat. Nanny's memory is a permanent reminder to me that being a party pooper is often the most loving thing I can do.

Saying ''I told you so'' is no substitute for a loving no.

Pollyanna in a Rocking Chair

Do everything without complaining or arguing, so that you may be innocent and pure as God's perfect children, who live in a world of corrupt and sinful people.

—*Philippians 2:14-15*

SEVENTEEN

I've always jokingly said that I was going to end up as a cranky old lady who sat in her rocking chair and whined continually to all and sundry.

The picture was meant to be humorous, but I have a nagging suspicion that my whining is increasing proportionally with my age. You'd think that it would be the other way around, that I'd finally reach a stage when I realized that what you see is what you get. But no, the older I grow, the more susceptible I am to a disease called the WWM's.

The WWM's are the Whingey, Whiney, Moaney's, a phrase coined by me many years ago to describe a cranky three-year-old son. It also describes an equally cranky adult.

I once worked at a large tourist facility that was created simply for people to visit and enjoy. To an outsider looking in, it looked like the ideal place to pursue a career. But inside, the WWM's had taken hold. It's the kind of disease that turns everything sour. If you happened to comment that it was a lovely sunny day, someone would be bound to complain that it was drying out the lawns and now we'd have to put on extra sprinklers, and that would mean more workers, and the budgets had been cut again, and they didn't know how anyone could expect them to carry on an operation if they couldn't bring in more workers when they were needed, and if management had to spend ten minutes in the field, they'd soon realize that operations required a stable budget. . . . The day didn't look so nice after all.

And if you should say that the sales were up and wasn't that great, someone would say, more sales means we have to get in more stock, and now we'll have to take some people off the salesfloor to get up there and sort out the stockroom before we can get more stock out on the floor, and if the whole system was properly computerized like we suggested it should be last year, we wouldn't be in this mess now, and if management just listened to the advice of the people who actually had to run the business. . . . The sales didn't look so great after all.

The WWM's spoiled everything. Soon, no one could see anything good in anything, anywhere. Whatever happened, the negative effects were immediately discussed; there were no positive factors. No wonder people become embittered, soured, disillusioned, and miserable. If left unchecked, the WWM's disease will continue on its destructive path until there is no joy left.

I have always thought of myself as a Pollyannaish optimist, but even the most optimistic person finds it difficult to fight off the WWM's. There is something instrinsically satisfying to my human nature to have something to whine about. It's as if all my worries and fears are justified, and I can let the world know it's just as bad as I suspected it would be.

I don't know why I find it so hard to let go of the WWM's. I have everything to be thankful for. I know the good news. I have seen that everything works together for good in my life. I am loved, cared for, part of a wonderful plan.

And yet, I continued to allow the disease to run rampant through my life. I whinge that I don't seem to have enough faith. I whine that God seems far away from me. I moan that life is unfair; that I don't have an easy time; that God isn't listening.

Then I wonder why my Christian life seems to be stunted. I feel bitter when I see the joy that other people have. Whinge, whine, moan.

What would happen if I became the cure—the antibiotic that freed people around me from the WWM's? What would happen if I allowed the joy of the Lord to wipe out the WWM's forever?

I might end up as a happy old Pollyanna in a rocking chair! Now that's a future I can look forward to on the other side of the hill!

ABOUT THE AUTHOR

Patricia Wilson lives on Potluck Farm in rural Ontario, Canada, with her husband and children. She has had a wide variety of jobs and occupations and is currently a business counsellor in a provincial self-help center for small businesses.

Ms. Wilson is involved in the civic and religious lives of her community. She is also the author of *Too Much Holly, Not Enough Holy?*, *Have You Met My Divine Uncle George?*, *Who Put All these Cucumbers in My Garden?*, and *The Daisies Are Still Free*.